ESSENTIAL THEMES

Thought Starters for Special Occasions

By

KEITH L. BROOKS

MOODY PRESS
CHICAGO

Formerly entitled
Fifty Essential Themes

Revised Edition, 1974

ISBN: 0-8024-2384-1

Printed in the United States of America

"What Can I Say?"

"LISTEN, BILL, can we count on you for a ten-minute talk at our brotherhood meeting?"

"Who? *ME?* What could *I* talk about? I just *couldn't* do it, Jim. I'm no speaker. Get somebody else!"

Isn't that about what happens when a good chance to witness for the Lord comes along? It isn't that you *can't talk.* You do *lots* of talking. It is just that you do not know how to prepare a message. You have no good material saved up. If you just had some IDEAS, some fitting scripture passages, and a few good illustrations, you could tackle it.

This set of themes is to help you meet such needs and to arm you with a fairly good range of appropriate subjects. Each is complete in itself for at least a ten-minute talk, but the scripture passages are almost certain to bring to mind personal experiences and illustrations to expand the message somewhat.

If you will take any of these themes and use it according to the pointers given on the following page, you may be certain, when you sit down, that you have said something WORTHWHILE and you will have no reason to have any sense of defeat.

Do not say no to a good opportunity to speak for Christ. The next time it comes, pick a fitting topic and GO TO IT.

Pointers

These lessons, you will notice, are in a convenient note size. In case you wish to add to these outlines, we suggest that you clip a blank sheet of paper to the page opposite the lesson you use and, by arrows made with red pencil on the printed lesson, point to the paragraphs opposite which are to be inserted. This may save the necessity of a complete rewriting.

Master the notes if you have time, but, in any case, even if called upon on short notice, you need make no excuses. You are utilizing the Word of God, which is "quick and powerful"; and if you give your message *leisurely and thoughtfully,* you have provided your hearers with food for thought.

When introduced, step forward as one on business for the *King, stand up straight* and face the people. *Take time to fill your lungs with air.* This will give you self-possession. *Be yourself.* Look the people *in the eyes* and go ahead.

Make no apologies whatsoever. Give them a complete surprise. Start talking. Note that each message opens with *a pointed statement* to gain attention. *Make it emphatic* and speak clearly— *loud enough to be heard by all.*

Keep your shoulders up and *keep breathing* to the bottom of your lungs. Take your time. *Don't lean on anything* and *don't put your hands in your pockets.*

Don't fizzle out. You have something gripping to say so *keep going* and *don't allow your voice to drop down. Push for the climax.* Be determined that you are going to make every hearer take home with him the concrete idea back of your message.

Keep within the time allotted you. Take your seat with assurance that you have faithfully given out *God's Word* and that it will not return unto Him void.

4

Titles

1

Key of the Morning

ATTENTION-GETTER: THE BEST WAY TO GET ON YOUR FEET IS TO GET ON YOUR KNEES.

Psalm 5:3 tells us when to begin: "My voice shalt thou hear in the morning, O Lord: In the morning will I direct my prayer unto thee, and will look up."

Matthew Henry: "Prayer is the key of the morning and the bolt of the evening."

Have YOU a "good morning" to greet our Lord? If we run from Him in the morning, we will have trouble finding Him the rest of the day.

David: "Cause me to hear thy loving kindness in the morning; for in thee do I trust: cause me to know the way wherein I should walk" (Psalm 143:8).

We need to get our DIRECTIONS at the day's BEGIN-NING—before our minds are flooded with other things.

Andrew Bonar (great man of prayer) had three rules: (1) not to speak to any *man* before speaking to *Jesus;* (2) not to do anything with his *hands* until he had been on his *knees;* (3) not to read the *papers* until he had read his *Bible.*

Jesus: "In the morning, rising up a great while before day, he went out and departed into a solitary place, and there prayed" (Mark 1:35).

Hudson Taylor, founder of China Inland Mission, was so pressed for time from the minute he got up in the morning, that he would set his alarm for 3:00 A.M. and, after spending an hour in devotions, would go back to bed.

SPIDERS, before seeking their prey in the morning, mend their broken webs. Shall we pursue the business of earth before we have concerned ourselves about the broken webs of life?

> The morning is the gate of day,
>   But, ere you enter there,
> See that you set to guard it well
>   The sentinel of prayer.
>
> ANNIE JOHNSON FLINT

2

The Prayer Period

There are 1440 minutes in a day: How many of them are given to prayer—five—ten?

Jesus: "But thou, WHEN thou prayest [suggesting a PERIOD], enter into thy CLOSET [suggesting RETIRE-MENT] . . . pray to thy FATHER which is in secret [the ANSWERER of prayer, a personal God]; and thy Father which seeth in secret shall REWARD thee openly" [the YIELD of prayer] (Matthew 6:6).

$$\left.\begin{array}{l} \text{P—eriod} \\ \text{R—etirement} \\ \text{A—nswerer} \\ \text{Y—ield} \end{array}\right\} = \text{PRAY}$$

Four points about prayer. (Go over them again)

The Bible clearly teaches the need of a SET TIME and PLACE for collection of thought, emptying of self, and a fresh touch of the Holy Spirit.

Evangelist John A. Davis: "God's acquaintance is not made by popping in on Him occasionally. He cannot bestow His best gifts upon hasty and irregular comers."

Daniel: "He went into the house and, his windows being open in his chamber toward Jerusalem, he kneeled down upon his knees three times a day and prayed and gave thanks before his God" (Daniel 6:10).

David: "Evening and morning, and at noon, will I pray, and cry aloud: and he shall hear my voice" (Psalm 55:17).

Peter: "Peter went up upon the housetop to pray about the sixth hour" (Acts 10:9).

We are to be CONSTANTLY in a spirit of prayer: "Pray without ceasing" (1 Thessalonians 5:17); "Men ought ALWAYS to pray and not to faint" (Luke 18:1)— BUT a special PERIOD of solitude with God is NECESSARY.

The Reverend Cornelius Wolfekin, noted preacher of past days, found his labors barren. His wife suggested it might be due to lack of a prayer PERIOD. They entered into a pact. Each should have an hour alone in the morning. It was the beginning of great blessing upon his ministry. So it may be for you.

3

The Relation of Prayer to Service

ATTENTION GETTER: THE PEOPLE WHO ARE USED OF GOD IN PUBLIC ARE THE ONES WHO HAVE FIRST MET HIM IN PRIVATE.

Let us link together TWO passages:

1. One with Christ, we appear *in the presence of God*— "And *whatsoever* ye shall ASK *in my name,* that will I do that the Father may be glorified in the Son" (John 14:13).

NOTE: We have no approach to God except on the basis of what CHRIST is to us.

2. Also one with Christ, we are to appear *before the WORLD*—"And *whatsoever* ye DO in word or deed, DO all *in the name of the Lord Jesus,* giving thanks to God and the Father through him" (Colossians 3:17).

NOTE: If one is borrowing from the bank, the name of a creditable person is required as an endorser of the note. Out of gratitude to this person, we would certainly not be ashamed to be IDENTIFIED with him *before our friends* and would wish to do him every kindness possible.

Through PRAYER, we draw upon heaven's bank only through the *standing* we have in Christ—"My God shall supply all your need according to his riches in glory by *Christ Jesus*" (Philippians 4:19).

It is only through HIM that the believer is ENABLED for ALL things—"I can DO all things *through Christ which strengtheneth me*" (Philippians 4:13).

Should we not give all honor unto that name which has entitled us to draw upon the riches of glory—serving Him openly and gladly?

Our two passages suggest that PRAYER *in His name* is intended to be a promoter of ACTIVITY *in His name.*

PRAYER puts one at HIS DISPOSAL and enables one in all he DOES to bring glory to His name.

You say you PRAY in His name. DO YOU WORK in His name and for His glory?

Let not prayer be a substitute for SERVICE. Let there be no service that is not the outcome of PRAYER.

4

According to His Will

ATTENTION-GETTER: SOME GO TO PRAYER NOT TO SEEK GOD'S WILL BUT TO ASK HIM TO BACK UP WHAT *THEY WILL* TO DO.

1 John 5:14-15: "This is the *confidence* we have in HIM, that if we ask anything *according to his will*, he heareth us. And *if we know* that he hear us, whatsoever we ask, *we know* that we HAVE the petitions we desired of him."

This PRAYER PROMISE clearly suggests the possibility that a Christian may have GUIDANCE in prayer—so that he will RECEIVE *the very thing* asked.

NOTE THE WORD *"confidence."* How does one get real assurance in prayer? There must be a feeling that his prayer is the very ECHO of God's will. Then he KNOWS that the answer is coming even before it is in sight.

What is the KEY to gaining this ASSURANCE? Ephesians 6:18: "Praying always with all prayer and supplication IN THE SPIRIT [in full yieldedness to the Spirit] and *watching thereunto* with all perseverance and supplication."

DO WE TAKE TIME to seek the Spirit's guidance in our ASKING? Turn to Romans 8:26: "The Spirit helpeth our infirmities [in prayer]: for WE know not WHAT we should pray for as we ought."

Again in Jude 19: "Building up yourself in the most holy faith, PRAYING IN [or in surrender to] the HOLY SPIRIT."

Oswald Chambers: "There is a quiet ANTEROOM of PRAYER in which we may hear IN ADVANCE the prayer GOD would have us pray, and this prayer will be according to His will."

WHERE is this ANTEROOM? It is in the place where we let the HOLY SPIRIT dictate to our hearts what we should say in prayer. Psalm 27:14: "WAIT, I SAY, ON THE LORD."

An old Naval rule: When ships are to readjust their compasses, they must drop anchor in some QUIET SPOT. WE MUST quiet ourselves to God's presence before we can learn to PRAY BETTER PRAYERS—prayers that MUST be ANSWERED, because they are the echo of HIS will.

5

The Believer's Welfare with Temptation

ATTENTION-GETTER: YOU CAN'T KEEP BIRDS FROM FLYING OVER YOUR HEAD, BUT YOU CAN PREVENT THEM FROM BUILDING NESTS IN YOUR HAIR.

1 Corinthians 10:12-13: "Let him that thinketh he standeth take heed lest he fall. There hath no temptation taken you but such as is common to man, but *God is faithful,* who will not suffer you to be tempted above that ye are able; but will with the temptation also make a way to escape, that ye may be able to bear it."

We only need Genesis 3 to learn that the best surroundings conceivable CAN'T make one proof against temptation (modern fallacies: convent walls, ideal environment, etc.).

WHY? It is because (1) man has WITHIN him a corrupt NATURE susceptible to evil suggestion (James 1:14) and (2) there is a *devil* to put pressure on him *from without* (1 Peter 5:8).

PROF. DRUMMOND thought he could escape by going into the heart of Africa; but alone in the jungle, he met up with satanic suggestions. ST. ANTHONY, in his cave, saw the loathsome face of the devil.

THE VERY FACT that ALL ARE TEMPTED shows God has a PURPOSE. What can it be?

1. James 1:2-4: "My brethren, count it all joy when ye fall into [lit., when ye are hedged in by] divers temptations; knowing this, that the trying of your faith worketh patience. But let patience have her perfect work, that ye may be perfect [mature] and entire, wanting nothing."

2. James 1:12: "Blessed is the man that endureth temptation: for when he is tried, he shall receive the crown of life, which the Lord hath promised to them that love him."

NOTE: You CAN'T make an athlete by shutting a man in an empty gymnasium with nothing to put his muscles to the test. TEMPTATION IS THE FRICTION NECESSARY TO DEVELOPMENT.

HOW DO WE OVERCOME? James 4:7: "*Submit* yourselves therefore to God. *Resist* the devil and he will *flee from you.*" Ephesians 6:13: "*Take unto you* the whole armor of God that ye may be able to *withstand* in the evil day, and having done all, to *stand*" a VICTOR in the name of the conquering Lord!

6

The Why of Trouble for the Christian

ATTENTION-GETTER: A CHRISTIAN IS A PER-SON WHOM GOD HAS UNDER TREATMENT.

David: "Before I was *afflicted* I went astray, *but now* have I kept thy word . . . It is *good for me* that I have been afflicted; that I might *learn thy statutes*" (Psalm 119:67, 71).

Even the CHRISTIAN, by natural tendency, is ready to wander at times out of God's will. AFFLICTIONS become the guide to REFLECTION and the parent of REPENT-ANCE (Paul's prayer—Philippians 3:10).

Many when hemmed in by troubles *begin to ask WHY.* God's Word alone can give us the ANSWERS.

1. *PROOF of our spiritual state.* We have been putting up a good *religious front;* but actually, *how deep* has the heart entered into His fellowship? How much can our faith stand? (See 1 Peter 1:6-7.)

To Israel: "Thou shalt remember all the way which the Lord thy God led thee these forty years in the wilderness, to humble thee, and to PROVE thee, *to know what was in thine heart,* whether thou wouldst keep his command-ments, or no" (Deuteronomy 8:2).

Job, after his testings: "I have heard of thee by the *hear-*

16

ing of the ear, **BUT NOW** mine *eye seeth thee"* (Job 42: 5).

Sharp trials are to the soul like a *soaking rain* to a house. We discover *where the leaks are* in the roof and where to *make repairs.* Our RESOLUTION: Job 23:10.

2. *POLISHER of character.* James 1:3-4 *"Knowing* this, that the *trying of your faith* worketh patience, but let patience have her *perfect work,* that ye may be perfect and entire, wanting nothing." (Also Hebrews 12:7-11)

Many Christian graces—patience, humility, resignation, meekness, etc.—*can't thrive without trials.* Blows to the *outward man* produce eternal effects in the *inner man.*

Count each affliction *God's messenger* sent to YOU and be not impatient for a *quick deliverance.* Wait *God's time.* Count on 2 Corinthians 4:17-18 and Romans 8:18, 28.

7

God's Plan of Salvation

ATTENTION-GETTER: An old negro lady said, "AH WANTS TO GIT RELIGION, BUT AH DREADS DE PROCESS."

That is a false notion many have. God has put His plan of salvation by GRACE on a level where ALL can easily get it. The Spirit of God responds to SIMPLE FAITH.

1. *JESUS BOUGHT IT.* Matthew 20:28: "The Son of man came not to be ministered unto, but to minister, and to give his life a RANSOM for many." 1 Peter 1:18-19: "Ye were not redeemed with corruptible things, as silver and gold . . . but with the precious blood of Christ, as of a lamb without blemish and without spot."

THIS MEANS that Jesus died as our SUBSTITUTE and gave His precious life to settle the sinner's debt to God. Had not the Lamb of God (John 1:29) taken our place, HELL would have been the alternative for all those who come short of the glory of God.

2. *THE WORD TAUGHT IT.* God found a way to reveal His universal PLAN through the *written Word,* translated and passed on from age to age. John 20:31: "These are written that ye might believe that Jesus is the Christ,

the Son of God; and that believing ye might have life through his name."

We have the privilege of pointing out to our fellow men this divine message of eternal life.

3. *FAITH SOUGHT IT*. Ephesians 2:8: "For by GRACE [unmerited favor] are ye saved through FAITH: and that not of yourselves: it is the GIFT of God: not of works." John 1:12: "As many as received HIM, to them gave he power to become the sons of God, even to them that believe on his name."

Thus the GIFT of ETERNAL LIFE is made *easily available to ALL*. ACCEPT HIM in *simple childlike faith* and see what happens.

4. *THE HOLY SPIRIT WROUGHT IT*. Titus 3:5: "NOT by works of righteousness which WE have done, but according to his mercy he saved us, by the washing of regeneration and the renewing of the Holy Spirit."

"Except a man be born [FROM ABOVE (lit.)] he cannot see the kingdom of God" (John 3:3).

8

The Books God Writes

ATTENTION-GETTER: DID YOU KNOW THAT
GOD IS STILL WRITING BOOKS?

Psalm 19 shows that God makes Himself known to men
through THREE BOOKS of His own writing: (1) vv. 1-
6, the book of nature; (2) vv. 7-11, the book of the written Word; (3) vv. 12-14, the book of human life.

1. The BOOK OF NATURE—*God's PRIMER for all
people. "The heavens declare the glory of God;* and the fir-
mament sheweth his handiwork" (v. 1). THEME: the
Glory, Handiwork, Knowledge of the Creator.

Romans 1:12: "The invisible things of him from the
creation of the world are *clearly seen,* being understood by
the *things that are made,* even his eternal power and Godhead, so that men are *without excuse."*

Language of the Book—"Day unto day it uttereth [gives
out] speech [the silent voice of nature] and night unto
night sheweth knowledge" (Psalm 19:2). *Scope of the
Book*—"Their line is gone out through all the earth, and
their words to the end of the world" (v. 3).

2. The BOOK OF THE WRITTEN WORD—*God's
ACADEMY. "The law of the* LORD *is perfect, converting
the soul:* the *testimony of the* LORD *is* sure, making wise

20

the simple. The *statutes of the* LORD are right, rejoicing the heart: *The commandment of the* LORD is pure, enlightening the eyes. More to be desired are they than gold, yea, than much fine gold: sweeter also than honey and the honeycomb" (vv. 7-10). THEME: the *Glory, Handiwork, Knowledge* of the heavenly Father.

Language of the Book—The voice of the Holy Spirit. *Scope of the Book*—"Whosoever" will believe (John 1: 12). "By them [God's testimonies] is thy servant warned: and in keeping of them there is great reward" (Psalm 19: 11).

3. The BOOK OF HUMAN LIFE—*the GRADUATED PRODUCT. Every redeemed soul, an epistle* of Christ which others read. ARE WE READABLE CHRISTIANS? "Cleanse thou me from secret faults. Keep back thy servant also from presumptuous sins; let them not have dominion over me. . . . Let the words of my mouth," etc. (vv. 12-14). THEME: the *Glory of God* revealed in us. *Scope of the Book*—(Philippians 2:15-16).

Are these three books in harmony?

21

9

A Searching Prayer

Psalm 139:23-24

ATTENTION-GETTER: SIN IS THE GREATEST OF ALL DETECTIVES: BE SURE IT WILL FIND YOU OUT.

"Search ME, O God, and know my *heart:* try me, and know my *thoughts.* And see if there be any wicked *way* in me, and lead me in the way everlasting" (Psalm 139:23-24).

NOTE THREE THINGS in David's attitude: (1) *self-examination*—"search *me . . .* try *me*"; (2) *self-renunciation*—He confesses the weakness of the self life, "wicked way in me"; (3) *self-dedication*—"lead me in the way everlasting."

THREE THINGS ASKED:

1. "SEARCH me": he believed that God, by His omnipresence, was aware of every evil tendency in him. He wanted God to *make HIM conscious* of any hindrance to divine blessing.

2. "TRY me" (lit., "test me as metals are proven in a furnace") : having invited scrutiny, he now says, "Lord, do

22

anything with me that will make for my purification." *Dare we pray thus* (1 Peter 1:7)?

3. "LEAD me": he recognizes that it is *not in man* to lead himself aright. *"The way everlasting"* is not according to the natural mind. We *must* be LED in it.

THREE SEATS OF TROUBLE: (1) *"know my HEART"*—the workshop where we plan all our doings; (2) "know my THOUGHTS"—the half-finished product of sin: what we THINK when we are alone shows what we ARE at heart; (3) "see if there be any *wicked WAY*"— *the course of life,* finished product, formed habits, etc.

THREE IMPORTANT QUESTIONS:

1. Are we conscious of *lack of power?*

2. Do we want to be *more used of God?*

3. Are we ready to *pray through to victory?*

The course to take: Proverbs 28:13—"Whoso covereth his sins shall not prosper: whoso confesseth and forsaketh them shall have mercy"; 1 John 1:9—"If we confess our sins, he is faithful and just to forgive us our sins, and to cleanse us from unrighteousness."

Do we HONESTLY want to be more used of God?

10

The Threefold Ministry

Acts 3:1-12

ATTENTION-GETTER: IF WE CANNOT DO THE GOOD WE WOULD, WHAT'S THE REASON WE DO NOT DO THE GOOD WE CAN?

Peter and John, in the line of duty, came upon OPPORTUNITY (from *ob portus,* before a portal): a helpless man at the very gate of the temple. There are OPPORTUNITIES just outside our church door.

Let us see what they did.

1. *Ministry of the EYES* (Acts 3:4): "And Peter, fastening *his eyes upon* him with John, said: LOOK on us."

What do we see as we go along our way? Some look with CURIOSITY (John 9:2), some with CONTEMPT (Luke 10:31-32), some with COMPASSION (Luke 10:33).

2. *Ministry of the LIPS* (Acts 3:6): "Then Peter *said* [the LIPS]. Silver and gold have I none: but [what] I have give I thee: In the name of Jesus Christ of Nazareth rise up and walk."

All our *prayers* for evangelization are *bitter irony* when

24

our LIPS are sealed in *testimony for the Lord.* Psalm 35: 28: *"My tongue* shall SPEAK of thy righteousness and of thy praise *all the day long."*

Some say, "I LIVE my religion: I don't *talk* it." If we do not SPEAK for Christ, *who gets the credit* for our good living? SELF!

3. *Ministry of the HAND* (Acts 3:7): "And they took him by the right hand and LIFTED HIM UP: and immediately his feet and ankle bones received strength."

PRAY and PULL is the combination for helping people—RIGHT HAND OF FELLOWSHIP and POWER.

They learned this from JESUS (Mark 1:31): "He took her by the right hand and lifted her up."

RESULT (Acts 3:8): "And he leaping up stood, and walked, and entered with them into the temple, walking, and leaping, and praising God."

11

Bible Rules for Bible Study

ATTENTION-GETTER: "THE BIBLE IS THE WORD OF LIFE. I BEG YOU TO STUDY IT AND FIND THIS OUT FOR YOURSELF" Woodrow Wilson.

Believers in Berea—Acts 17:11—"These were more noble than those in Thessalonica, in that they received the word with all readiness of mind, and *searched* the scriptures daily, whether those things were so."

Acrostic on SEARCH

SYSTEMATICALLY. 2 Timothy 2:15—"Study to shew thyself approved unto God, a workman that needeth not to be ashamed, rightly dividing the word of truth."

DON'T use the GRASSHOPPER method of hop, skip, and jump through the Bible. Have a PLAN of study and *stick to it.*

EARNESTLY. Psalm 119:18—"Open thou mine eyes, that I may behold wondrous things out of thy law."

Study *prayerfully,* seeking the GUIDANCE of the Holy Spirit, who inspired the writers. John 16:14—"He shall take of the things of mine and shew them unto you."

26

ANXIOUSLY. Psalm 119:27—"Make me to understand the *way of thy precepts*, so shall I talk of thy wondrous works."

Study with the purpose of *equipping yourself* to meet the assaults of Satan and to be *a help to others*.

REGULARLY. Psalm 1:2-3—"His delight is in the law of the LORD; and in his law doth he meditate day and night. And he shall be like a tree planted by the rivers of water, that bringeth forth his fruit in his season; his leaf also shall not wither; and whatsoever he doeth shall prosper."

Just as we need PHYSICAL NOURISHMENT at regular periods, so, if we are to be fruitful for God, we must have *regular seasons* for MEDITATION.

CAREFULLY. 2 Timothy 3:16-17—"All scripture is given by inspiration of God, and is profitable for *doctrine,* for *reproof,* for *correction,* for *instruction* in righteousness: that the man of God may be *perfect,* thoroughly furnished unto all good works."

Don't read it just to *cover ground,* but for *instruction.*

HUMBLY. Psalm 51:17—"A broken and a contrite heart, O God, thou wilt not despise."

God doesn't give his treasures to stubborn hearts. He loves to reveal His wonders to *humble* seekers.

12

Fishers of Men

ATTENTION-GETTER: LITTLE SENTENCES SPO-KEN SINCERELY FOR JESUS SAVE SOULS FOR ETERNITY.

Matthew 4:19—"Jesus saith unto them, Follow me, and I will make you fishers of men."

Here is (1) AN ESSENTIAL CONDITION—"follow me"— and (2) AN EXPECTED CONSUMMATION—"I will *make* you."

This plainly implies that ALL who truly follow Jesus are *under command* to be HIS WITNESSES: they should have a TESTIMONY to others.

OBSERVE THESE TWO POINTS:

1. *"Follow me."* This means first that one has come to Him for eternal life (John 3:16).

It also means that the saved one seeks to follow in His steps as a Christian—"for even hereunto were ye called: because Christ also suffered for us, leaving us an example, that ye should *follow his steps*" (1 Peter 2:21). Are you following?

Before one can effectively approach others, he must be a *consecrated* believer *himself*—able to say, with the psalmist, Psalm 40:2-3 (*read*).

28

2. *"I will make you fishers."* This is the expected consequence. He gives His true followers a sense of responsibility toward the unsaved about them.

2 Corinthians 5:20—"Now then we are ambassadors for Christ, as though *God* did beseech you *by us:* we pray you in Christ's stead, be ye reconciled to God."

EVERY CHRISTIAN'S LIFE WORK is FISHING for others. Making a LIVING is a sideline.

Seventy percent of all trade, we are told, comes through PERSONAL SALESMANSHIP.

Of forty specific cases recorded in the gospels, only six came to Jesus *of themselves. In twenty cases,* we are told, individuals were BROUGHT by someone.

CATCH FISH, one by one: this is JESUS' OWN PLAN. Along the way, every day, IT WILL PAY.

13

How We Grieve the Holy Spirit

ATTENTION-GETTER: IF WE WANT AN IN-
CREASE OF SPIRITUAL BLESSING, THERE MUST
BE A DECREASE OF SELF-WILL.

Ephesians 4:30—"Grieve not the Holy Spirit of God,
whereby ye are sealed unto the day of redemption."

The New Testament tells of TWO classes of SINS
against the Holy Spirit:

  1. those committed by UNBELIEVERS.
  2. those committed by SAVED PEOPLE.

1. *Unbelievers:* According to Matthew 12:31 one can
blaspheme the Holy Spirit to a point where salvation
would be *impossible* to him.

One may also *resist* the Holy Spirit (Acts 7:51) to a
point where he would have *no further desire* to be saved.

One may often *insult* the Holy Spirit (Hebrews 10:29).

2. CHRISTIANS can do TWO THINGS.

"QUENCH" the Spirit, 1 Thessalonians 5:19. This
means that, by trying to smother the leading of the Spirit
in their hearts (as one might try to quench a fire) they get
out of fellowship with God and come under His chasten-
ing.

GRIEVE the Spirit, Ephesians 4:30 *above*. That is, by allowing evil in their hearts, they forfeit their fellowship with God and become miserable.

In three ways BELIEVERS grieve the Spirit:

1. *By DISREGARDING His presence* in their hearts. 1 Corinthians 3:16—"Know ye not that ye are the temple of God, and that the Spirit of God dwelleth in you?"

The Holy Spirit is the inner Guest of every born-again person. What kind of a house do we keep for Him?

2. *By DISTRUSTING His Word about us.* He is the Author of the Bible promises. He is GRIEVED when we refuse to take Him at His Word.

3. *By DISREGARDING His command to us.* Ephesians 5:18—"BE FILLED."

We are God's property (1 Corinthians 6:19-20). We grieve Him most when we *will not let Him take control of His own property.*

True consecration is allowing the Holy Spirit to fill the house which God has purchased as His own.

14

Look unto Me and Be Ye Saved

Isaiah 45:22

ATTENTION-GETTER: THE DEVIL'S PARTICU-
LAR DELIGHT IS TO HAVE PEOPLE LOOK AT
THEIR OWN RIGHTEOUSNESS.

Three Important LOOKS of the New Testament

1. BACKWARD look to CALVARY. John 1:29—
"Behold the Lamb of God that taketh away the sin of the
world."

Remember: CHRIST saves us by doing FOR us and IN
our stead what we CANNOT do for ourselves. HE satis-
fies the demands of God's broken law on our behalf; He
paid ALL our debt. (Read John 3:36.)

2. UPWARD look to the THRONE. Hebrews 12:2—
"Looking unto Jesus, the *author* and *finisher* of our faith,
who for the joy that was set before him *endured the cross,*
despising the shame, and is set down at the right hand of
the throne of God."

Our RISEN Lord is our High Priest at the right hand of
God. (Read Hebrews 7:25). HE gives constant VIC-
TORY to those who "seek those things *which are above,*
where Christ sitteth on the right hand of God" (Colossians
3:1).

The BELIEVER looks to Him *day by day* (1) for guidance, (2) for heart searching, (3) for power to live on the heavenly level.

3. FORWARD look to His *coming again.* Titus 2:13— *"Looking for* that blessed hope, and the glorious appearing of the great God and our Saviour [or, of our great God and Saviour] Jesus Christ."

This is our *purifying hope.* 1 John 3:3—"Every man that hath *this hope in him,* purifieth himself, even as he is pure."

By ever looking FORWARD to His return (a) we try *to live* as we would like to be found living when He comes; (b) we seek to *win others* so as to hasten the completion of the mystical body of Christ, the elect number; and (c) we are assured that all *our service* may be *intelligent* and *enduring.*

SUMMARY: Have YOU yet taken that first LOOK of faith toward the LAMB? If NOT, you can expect nothing from the throne and are "without hope" in the world.

15

Three Classes Among the Lost

ATTENTION-GETTER: THERE IS ONLY ONE LADDER TO HEAVEN—CALVARY'S CROSS.

In our WITNESSING for Christ, we will find THREE *types of people* for whom we *must* be armed with Scripture.

1. NEGLECTORS. Hebrews 2:3—"How shall *we* escape, if we *neglect* so *great* salvation?"

ALL one has to do to be ETERNALLY LOST is just to DO NOTHING about being saved. Keep on PUTTING OFF. John 3:18—"He that *believeth not* is condemned *already,* because he hath NOT believed in the name of the only begotten Son of God."

The devil's cleverest trick—ENGROSS ONE'S ATTENTION IN ANYTHING BUT THE ONE ESSENTIAL THING. Hell is paved with *good intentions.* Then come sickness or accident—and death: TOO LATE!

2. REJECTORS. Many think they are GOOD ENOUGH and *do not require anything* from Christ. They smugly declare, "I'll take my chances."

So thought many of the Jews. Paul said, "I bear them record that they have a ZEAL of God, but *not* according to *knowledge.* For they being *ignorant of GOD'S righteousness,* and going about to establish THEIR OWN righteousness, have not submitted themselves unto the right-eousness of God" (Romans 10:3).

We MUST take the WAY of salvation GOD has *decreed and provided.* We cannot stand in OUR OWN righteousness at His bar. (Read Titus 3:5; Isaiah 64:6.)

3. DESPISERS. Romans 2:4—*"Despiseth thou the riches of his goodness?"*

These people consider *themselves* WISER than those who wrote by divine inspiration. 1 Corinthians 3:19-20—"The wisdom of *this world* is *foolishness* with God. For it is written, he taketh *the wise* in their own craftiness. And again, The Lord knoweth the thoughts of the wise, that they are vain."

MANY such have come to face death in UTTER DE-SPAIR, BUT—quote John 1:12 and 16.

16

ABC's of Life

ATTENTION-GETTER: IF YOU COULD HAVE
MERITED YOUR SALVATION, IT WOULD NEVER
HAVE BEEN NECESSARY FOR JESUS TO DIE.

"ALL have sinned, and come short of the glory of God"
(Romans 3:23).

"BEHOLD the LAMB OF GOD, which taketh away the
sin of the world" (John 1:29).

"COME unto me, all ye that labour and are heavy laden,
and I will give you rest" (Matthew 11:28).

The Bible ABC's show us that (1) in ourselves we are
RUINED; (2) in Christ we are REDEEMED; and (3)
when we RECEIVE Christ, we are SAVED.

A. SIN has *ruined* ALL. Isaiah 53:6—"ALL we like
sheep have *gone astray;* we have turned EVERY ONE to
his own way; and the LORD hath laid on HIM [Jesus] the
iniquity of us ALL."

The fact of SIN in our natures *cannot be denied.* We are
"holden with the cords of [our] sins" (Proverbs 5:22).
"Behold, I was shapen in iniquity; and in sin did my
mother conceive me" (Psalm 51:5).

Consider the sins of a lifetime—in thought, act, and
omission. Only by *God's provision* can they be blotted out.

B. CHRIST has *redeemed* ALL. Galatians 3:13—
"Christ hath redeemed us from the curse of the law, being
made a curse for us." 1 Peter 2:24—He "bare our sins in
his own body on the tree."

This is the ONLY ANSWER to the sin problem. The
CROSS is the PLUS SIGN of our MINUS lives.

C. FAITH *saves* ALL who *receive Him.* John 6:37—
"Him that *cometh to me* I will in no wise cast out." John
1:12—To "as many as *receive him.*" Isaiah 44:22*b*—"*Return unto me;* for I have redeemed thee."

What does He say of those who RECEIVE? Isaiah 44:
22*a*—"I HAVE *blotted* out, as a thick cloud, thy transgressions."

What if TODAY *your* life should be cut off?

17

Law of the Harvest

ATTENTION-GETTER: LITTLE SINS ARE THE PIONEERS OF HELL.

Galatians 6:7-8—"Be not deceived; *God is not mocked:* for *whatsoever* a man soweth, *that* shall he also reap. For he that *soweth to his flesh* shall of the flesh reap corruption; but he that *soweth to the Spirit* shall of the Spirit reap life everlasting."

NOTE the TWO important facts about a HARVEST: (1) there is a law of QUALITY—*"whatsoever"*—like begets like; and (2) there is a law of QUANTITY—seed produces a CROP, in some instances a *tremendous increase.* Causes and effects are vitally linked. *II Cor 9:6*

These laws apply in the SPIRITUAL REALM as well as in the natural.

1. WHAT are you sowing? If to the FLESH, you will reap TWO kinds of corruption: (a) INWARD depravity and (b) OUTWARD wickedness.

"Sow a thought—reap a word. Sow a word—reap an act. Sow an act—reap a habit. Sow a habit—reap a character. Sow a character—reap a DESTINY."

This is as certain as the fact that the seed you plant will produce *"after its kind."* WHAT ARE YOU LIVING FOR?

38

2. WHAT of the *harvest time? How much* will you reap?

The creeping plume thistle multiplies so fast that, if all seeds were productive, the second crop would nearly cover the earth.

The eggs of a Gypsy moth, blown from a college professor's window, developed into adult moths which ravaged New England's trees. It has cost many thousands of dollars to fight them.

SIN sets in motion a train of causes leading to *increasingly disastrous effects.* Who knows what the harvest of one sin may be?

God's laws of the harvest CANNOT be mocked.

18

Salvation in Three Tenses

ATTENTION-GETTER: THE GOSPEL NOT ONLY SAVES FROM HELL BUT DELIVERS FROM THE THINGS THAT TAKE PEOPLE TO HELL.

SALVATION—*the great inclusive word* of the gospel—covers *all the redemptive processes.*

1. *We ARE saved* through faith in the atoning work of Jesus Christ—His DEATH on the cross. This is the PAST TENSE of Salvation.

2. We are BEING KEPT saved through the power of His risen life at the throne. This is the PRESENT TENSE.

3. We SHALL BE *completely delivered* into His very presence at death—and more fully when He comes in glory. This is the FUTURE TENSE.

Thus, we ARE saved, we are BEING saved, and we SHALL BE completely saved.

We talk of the *finished* work of Christ (John 17:4; but, ALL the work of Christ is ESSENTIAL in order to bring us, in glorified BODIES and fully rewarded, into the *final* heavenly state.

The Scriptures clearly indicate the three tenses of our salvation experience:

1. "Christ HATH redeemed us from the curse of the

40

law, being made a curse for us" (Galatians 3:13). "By grace ye ARE saved" (Ephesians 2:8). "Thy faith HATH saved thee" (Luke 7:50). "By him all that believe ARE justified from all things" (Acts 13:39). *Salvation Experienced.*

2. "If, when we were enemies, we were reconciled to God by the DEATH of his Son, much more, being reconciled, we SHALL BE [kept] saved by his LIFE" (Romans 5:10). "He is able also to save them TO THE UTTERMOST [limit of time] that come unto God by him, seeing he ever liveth to make intercession for them" (Hebrews 7:25). LOOKING unto Jesus (Hebrews 12:1-2) we are BEING SANCTIFIED (set apart unto Him more and more). *Salvation Progressing.*

3. "Now is our salvation nearer than when we believed" (Romans 13:11). We "are kept by the power of God through faith . . . *ready to be revealed in the last time*" (1 Peter 1:5). "Unto them that look for him shall he appear the second time without sin unto salvation" (Hebrews 9:28). This includes the body (Philippians 3:20-21). *Salvation Consummated.*

THE BEST IS YET TO COME.

41

19

The Logical Necessity of Salvation

ATTENTION-GETTER: NO ONE WILL EVER HAVE TO INSTITUTE A LAW SUIT TO COLLECT THE WAGES OF SIN.

Christians are absolutely CERTAIN that apart from Christ *there is no salvation:* "for there is none other name under heaven given among men, whereby we MUST be saved" (Acts 4:12). Let us consider an ACROSTIC on the letters of this word, *must.*

M stands for the MANDATORY salvation provided by God. *Said Jesus,* "Marvel not that I said unto you, ye MUST be born again" (John 3:7). "I am the way, the truth, and the life: NO MAN cometh unto the Father, but by ME" (John 14:6).

   God has the right to make the terms of salvation. They MUST be regarded. *Paul,* in Galatians 1:11, states, "I certify you . . . that the gospel which was preached of me is NOT AFTER MAN."

U stands for YOU—and all others—because "ALL have sinned, and come short of the glory of God" (Romans 3:23). "There is *none* righteous, no, not one" (v. 10). They are *all* gone out of the way, they are *together* become unprofitable; there is *none* that doeth good, *no, not one"* (v. 12).

42

S stands for the SON of God, the only *SAVIOUR. He alone* can provide a sufficient SACRIFICE. John 20: 31—"These are written, that ye might believe that Jesus is the Christ, the Son of God; and that *believing* ye might have life through his name." John 3:36—"He that *believeth* on the Son *hath* everlasting life: and he that *believeth* not the Son *shall not see life;* but the wrath of God abideth on him" (also 1 John 5:11-13).

T stands for TODAY, which is the TIME. 2 Corinthians 6:2—"I have heard thee in a TIME accepted: . . . now *is the accepted time;* behold, NOW is the day of salvation." Hebrews 3:7-8—"TO DAY if ye will hear his voice, harden not your hearts."

We have no lease on TOMORROW. Isaiah 55:6— "Seek ye the Lord WHILE HE MAY BE FOUND, call ye upon him WHILE HE IS NEAR." You cannot afford to trifle with God's "MUST."

20

Three Great Musts of Salvation

ATTENTION-GETTER: THERE IS A GREAT DIF-
FERENCE BETWEEN TURNING OVER A NEW
LEAF AND GETTING A NEW LIFE.

The basic message of the New Testament is that *human
reformation* will not take a soul to heaven: there *must* be
a recognition of the *divine redemption.* I would call your
attention to *three* great "MUSTS."

1. MUST OF REDEMPTION. Matthew 16:21—
"From that time forth began Jesus to show unto his disciples, how that he MUST go unto Jerusalem, and suffer
many things of the elders and chief priests and scribes, and
be killed, and be raised again the third day."

Jesus came not simply to PREACH but that there might
BE A GOSPEL TO PREACH—salvation through divine
ATONEMENT for sin. (Read 1 Peter 1:18-19).

We are SOLD under SIN (Romans 7:14). The Re-
deemer *had* to bear the curse of sin for us (Galatians 3:
13).

2. MUST OF REGENERATION. John 3:7—"Marvel
not that I said unto you, YE MUST be born *again.*"

IF this is *God's ordained way* to salvation—as all Scripture shows—then WE MUST seek this experience. The

44

TERMS are given in John 1:12-13: "As many as received him, to them gave he power to become the sons of God, even to them that BELIEVE ON HIS NAME: which were *born,* not of blood, nor of the will of the flesh, nor of the will of man, BUT OF GOD."

3. MUST OF PERSONAL RECEPTION. John 3:14-15—"As Moses lifted up the serpent in the wilderness, even so MUST the Son of man be lifted up: that WHOSO-EVER BELIEVETH in him should not perish, but have eternal life."

REJECTING *means just one thing:* John 3:18—"He that believeth NOT is *condemned already,* because he hath NOT believed in the name of the only begotten Son" (John 3:18) and "He that BELIEVETH NOT the Son shall NOT see life; but the *wrath of God abideth on him"* (v. 36).

TO BE LOST, all one has to do is to DISREGARD these three MUSTS.

21

Who Is the Christian?

ATTENTION-GETTER: MORAL LIFE MAY BE-
LONG TO ANY MAN, BUT SPIRITUAL AND ETER-
NAL LIFE BELONG ONLY TO THOSE WHO TAKE
GOD'S WAY OF SALVATION.

There is no salvation unless GOD HIMSELF has laid
down the terms of it. What says His divine Word?

1. A CHRISTIAN is one saved by the GRACE of God.
Ephesians 2:8-9—"For by *grace* are ye saved *through faith;*
and that not of yourselves: it is the *gift of God:* not of
works, lest any man should boast." Titus 3:5—"Not by
works of righteousness which we have done, but *according
to his mercy* he saved us, by the washing of regeneration,
and the renewing of the Holy Ghost."

D. L. Moody, the great evangelist, ran after a man, saying, "Do you know GRACE?" "Grace WHO?" the man
inquired. *"The Grace of God* that saves our souls!" Moody
answered, as he told him of the plan of salvation.

2. A CHRISTIAN is one redeemed by the BLOOD of
Christ.

2 Corinthians 5:19—"God was in Christ reconciling
the world unto himself." 1 Peter 1:19—We are *redeemed
"with the precious blood of Christ,* as of a lamb without

46

blemish and without spot." Isaiah 53:5-6—"He was wounded for our transgressions, he was bruised for our iniquities. . . . The LORD *hath laid on him* the iniquity of us all."

This was *God's provision* for meeting the SIN problem and taking from man's heart the burden of condemnation. "He that believeth on [the Son] is NOT condemned: but he that believeth not is condemned already" (John 3:18).

3. A CHRISTIAN is one sealed by the Spirit.

Ephesians 1:13-14—"In whom ye also trusted, after that ye heard the word of truth, the gospel of your salvation: in whom also after that ye believed, ye were *sealed with that holy Spirit* of promise, which is the earnest of our inheritance *until the redemption of the purchased possession,* unto the praise of his glory." The Christian is SECURED by the stamp of the Holy Spirit *until* the resurrection day—Romans 8:22-23. SOUGHT by the Father—SAVED by the blood of the Son—SEALED by the Spirit.

22

What Happens to a Backslider?

ATTENTION-GETTER: THE CHRISTIAN WHO HARBORS SECRET SIN IN HIS LIFE IS LOOKING FOR TROUBLE.

1 John 1:8-9—"If we say that we have no sin, we deceive ourselves, and the truth is not in us. If we *confess our sins,* he is faithful and just to forgive us our sins, and to cleanse us from all unrighteousness."

When a TRUE CHRISTIAN sins, WHAT HAPPENS?

1. *His FELLOWSHIP with God is severed. David,* when backslidden, mourned, "Day and night thy hand was heavy upon me: my moisture is turned into the drought of summer" (Psalm 32:4).

As CLOUDS hide the sun for days, so SIN comes between the soul and God.

2. *The JOY of salvation is lost.* One loses all relish for spiritual things: the heart is empty. David, in this condition, confessed, "My sin is ever before me" and "Restore unto me the joy of thy salvation; and uphold me with thy free Spirit" (Psalm 51:3, 12).

3. *Power for service is lost.* The Holy Spirit's power is ESSENTIAL for any real witness for Christ. It cannot be FAKED. *David* prayed, "Thou desirest truth in the inward

parts" and "Create in me a clean heart, O God; and renew a right spirit within me" (Psalm 51:6, 10).

4. *The Christian invites divine chastisement.* Hebrews 12:6-7—"Whom the Lord loveth he chasteneth, and scourgeth every son whom he receiveth. . . . What son is he whom the father chasteneth not?" Psalm 89:32-33— "I will visit their transgression with the rod, and their iniquity with stripes. Nevertheless, my lovingkindness will I not utterly take from him, nor suffer my faithfulness to fail."

5. *There is loss of reward.* (Read 1 Corinthians 3:11-15.) Out of FELLOWSHIP means out of SERVICE— out of service means that one is *failing to lay up treasures in heaven.* He is building of "wood, hay and stubble" which cannot endure the test of the rewarding day (1 Corinthians 3:12-15). Many will be chagrined in that day by suffering LOSS of REWARD.

TAKE THE WAY BACK NOW. Psalm 32:5; 1 John 1:9.

23

The Resource of the Christian

ATTENTION-GETTER: THE CALL OF GOD TO ANY PIECE OF WORK IS THE GUARANTEE THAT HE WILL BE THE RESOURCE OF ALL NEEDED STRENGTH.

Isaiah 40:31—"They that WAIT UPON the LORD shall *renew* [lit., exchange] their strength; they shall *mount up* with wings as eagles; they shall *run,* and not be weary; and they shall *walk,* and not faint."

The KEY is in the word translated "WAIT." The original word means " *to bind or twist"*—as rope is made by *intertwining*—so meaning *"to be closely bound up with* the Lord."

This is *something more than just attending meetings or saying prayers.* Do we really *CLING* unto the Lord?

HERE ARE THE RESULTS:

1. RISING—*"mount up."* Spiritual *UPLIFTING* causes the Christian to be not content anymore with the LOW LEVELS. He can now *soar above* the trials and burdens of life, *as eagles* built for *swift flight* in the *higher altitudes.*

2. RUNNING—*"run and not be weary."* Life is not all spiritual exhilaration. There's *a strenuous race* to be run in everyday life (1 Corinthians 9:24-26).

The RACE of life *brings weariness,* but CLINGING to the Lord brings an *exchange of our weakness* for heavenly power (Philippians 4:13).

3. ROUTINE—*"they shall WALK and not faint."* Walking lacks the exhilaration of the race course. The soldier in his MARCHING often faints. *The humdrum tasks* of life sap one's strength.

BUT, through *prayer "in every thing"* (Philippians 4: 6-7), we find ourselves *made adequate.*

DO WE KNOW that *supernatural power* that enables us for (1) spiritual RISING, (2) strenuous RUNNING, (3) steady ROUTINE?

Psalm 27:14—*"Wait on the* LORD: be of good courage, and he shall strengthen thine heart: WAIT, I SAY, ON THE LORD."

24

The Lost Bible

ATTENTION-GETTER: (hold up a Bible) "IS THERE ANYONE HERE WHO HAS LOST A BIBLE? ARE YOU SURE?

Read the story of 2 Chronicles 34:14-32.
THERE IS MORE THAN ONE WAY TO LOSE A BIBLE.

AN UNREAD Bible is a LOST Bible. One may have a Bible *in plain sight, yet it is lost* to him. Satan can't do his work where the Bible has its proper place.

The Bible is a MIRROR to reveal hearts (James 1:23-25). It is MILK to nourish the soul (1 Peter 2:2). It is a MOLD of character (Romans 6:17—word rendered "form" means "mold"). HOW ESSENTIAL ARE THESE THINGS!

HOW DO PEOPLE LOSE THEIR BIBLES?

1. DISREGARDING IT. *Satan has no end of devices* for drawing attention to everything else.

Patrick Henry, dying: "My greatest regret is that I never could find time to read my Bible. Now it is too late."
Moody: "I never yet saw a useful Christian who was NOT a student of the Bible."

Are YOU reading other books to the neglect of the

52

ONE BOOK? The number of words in the *Sunday newspaper* is usually more than the total number in the Bible.

2. DISOBEYING IT. Israel (2 Chronicles 34) drifted into worldly ways and *lost taste for spiritual things.* Either the Bible *keeps one from sin,* or sin *keeps one from the Bible.*

The Bible becomes distasteful when sin is loved (John 3:19). *Man's real quarrel* with the Bible is because he DOES NOT WANT to obey it.

3. DISTORTING IT. The Bible is lost to many today because of *the tamperings of men with it,* as they try to adapt it to shifting theories.

A little girl listened to a modernist preacher. Later she asked her mother, "Mother, was he FOR God or AGAINST HIM?"

HOW TO FIND A LOST BIBLE? *Meditate prayerfully upon it!* Psalm 1:2-3; Joshua 1:8; Psalm 119:11; Job 23:12.

25

Believers Out of Fellowship

ATTENTION-GETTER: THE SIN WE SPARE IS
THE SIN THAT WILL BECOME OUR MASTER.

A Japanese evangelist once illustrated a message by
spinning tops on the platform. He said, "Ministers have to
spend so much time *spinning up wobbly Christians,* they
can't get time to win the lost."

THREE KINDS OF BACKSLIDERS

1. DISOBEDIENT BELIEVERS—*Abraham in Egypt*
Genesis 12:10—"There was a famine in the land: and
Abram *went down into Egypt* to sojourn there." We are
most apt to be *tested just after seasons of great blessing.* It
is no sign we are in the wrong place just because famine
comes.

*Better to suffer in God's will than take things in your
own hands* and get into endless *complications.* See what
happened to Abram and Sara *until God intervened* and got
them out of Egypt.

2. DELUDED BELIEVERS—*Lot in Sodom*
Genesis 13:10-11—A man *seeking material things,* gets
spiritual blight. THREE STEPS DOWN: (a) *pitched
tent toward Sodom* (13:12)—watch out for *first leanings*

toward the world; (b) *dwelt in Sodom* (14:12)—trying to make the most of both worlds won't work; (c) *sat in the gate* (19:1)—He had gotten on in the world.

Not to be *OUT-AND-OUT* is to be *down-and-out*. Lot's *testimony gone,* he was *mocked* (19:14). God had to *drive him out* by the sorrows of earth. So it is with deluded Christians.

3. DISGRUNTLED BELIEVERS—*Peter by the Fire*

Luke 22:55-57. *Peter's feelings were hurt* when Jesus restored the ear he cut off (Luke 22:50-51; John 18:10). Now he *warms at the enemy's fire, after having followed afar off.*

BUT Peter was upheld by Jesus' prayer (Luke 22:32). See him later at another fire (John 21:9).

Are YOU out of place? Go back to the point where you took the DETOUR (1 John 1:9; Psalm 51:12).

JONAH
refusing
down
"
"
"
"
till 600

26

Stolen Property

ATTENTION-GETTER: GOD CAN DO WON-
DERS WHEN HE CAN GET THE USE OF HIS OWN
PROPERTY TO WORK WITH.

The focus-point of the Christian life is to recognize the
OWNERSHIP of the One who has BOUGHT us and
PAID FOR us.

1 Corinthians 6:19-20—"Know ye not that your body
is the temple of the Holy Ghost which is in you, which ye
have of God, and YE ARE NOT YOUR OWN? *For ye
are bought* with a price: *therefore* glorify God in your
body, and in your spirit, *which ARE GOD'S."*

TO WHOM DO I BELONG? That will settle all prob-
lems. CONSECRATION is simply *giving back* STOLEN
PROPERTY to its Owner—letting Christ have what right-
fully belongs to Him.

WE BEGIN by singing, "Give Me Jesus" and "Christ is
MINE." We should *go on* to say, "I AM HIS." (See Acts
27:23.)

WE BEGIN by *appropriation* of Christ. Have we gone
on to the PROPRIETORSHIP OF JESUS?

WE BEGIN with Jesus as *our Helper.* We must go on
to Jesus as our CONTROLLER. This *is* CONSECRA-
TION.

Romans 12:1—"I beseech you therefore, brethren, by the mercies of God, that ye PRESENT your bodies a living sacrifice, holy, acceptable unto God, which is your reasonable [LOGICAL] service." (The only logical thing we can do is recognize HIS ownership.)

CONSECRATION IS GOD *taking over and using His own property. Note the hymn: "Consecrate me* now to Thy service, Lord, *by the power of grace divine"* (second stanza of "Draw Me Nearer").

DEDICATION is OUR part: *taking hands off* that which does not belong to us, handing over to His control. CONSECRATION IS HIS PART.

This leads to TWO things in Romans 12:2: (1) *"Be not conformed* to this world (Moffatt translation of 1 Corinthians 7:31—"Let those who mix in the world live as if they were not engrossed in it"); (2) "But be ye transformed by the renewing of your mind." HOW? 2 Corinthians 3:18 (note that the word here translated "changed" is the same rendered "transformed" in Romans 12:2)— "EVEN AS BY THE SPIRIT."

27

The Spirit-Led Life

ATTENTION-GETTER: GOD IS READY TO HELP THE PERSON WHO HAS GOTTEN THROUGH WITH HIMSELF.

Romans 8:2—"The law of the Spirit of life in Christ Jesus hath made me free from the law of sin and death."

As the "Spirit of life," the Holy Spirit seeks to do *three things* for believers *who will submit* to Him:

1. ENABLE us to WORSHIP. Philippians 3:3—"We *worship God in the Spirit,* and rejoice in Christ Jesus, and have no confidence in the flesh."

To truly worship is to enter God's presence, but we are on earth and God is in heaven. HOW can we do it? In *full surrender* to the Holy Spirit. HE *makes us conscious of God's nearness* and brings the heart into the *spirit of devotion.*

Much that is stimulated by *psychological effects,* architecture, stained glass windows, lighting effects, etc., is NOT true WORSHIP.

2. EMPOWER us to PRAY. Ephesians 6:18—*"Praying always* with all prayer and supplication *in the Spirit."* Jude 20—"Praying *in the Holy Ghost."*

Are we channels through whom the Spirit can express *the will of God in prayer?* (See 1 John 5:14.)

58

Prayer life that is shut up to ONESELF falls easy prey to Satanic suggestions. Luke 18:11—"The Pharisee stood and prayed thus WITH HIMSELF"—note his prayer.

3. ENERGIZES us to WALK. Galatians 5:16—"*Walk in the Spirit,* and ye shall not fulfill the lust of the flesh."

We disarm the flesh, not by *self-repression* but by being *active in the higher sphere* in which the Holy Spirit directs us.

We hinder God by our own battling. Bring the Holy Spirit into the circumstances, and we experience *"the expulsive power of a new affection."* We walk in HIS energy.

28

The Three Crosses

ATTENTION-GETTER: THE CROSS OF JESUS IS THE PLUS SIGN OF OUR MINUS LIVES.

Luke 23:32—"There were also *two other* malefactors, led with him to be put to death."

Some time earlier, Jesus had been *on the mountain* between *two of the choicest saints* of heaven (Matthew 17:1-3).

But He had come "to seek and to save the lost"; so in THIS hour, we find Him DYING between two condemned SINNERS—one of whom became the *first trophy* of His redeeming love (Luke 23:42).

✝
Rejection
Sin IN him and ON him
    John 3:36

        ✝
      Redemption
    No sin IN HIM—1 John 3:5
    Sin laid ON Him—Isaiah 53:6
            ✝
          Reception
        Sin removed from him through faith
           Romans 4:7-8

1. A SINNER CONFESSED HIS SINS BEFORE GOD and man. Luke 23:40-41—this malefactor *rebuked the unbelieving* malefactor who railed against Jesus, reminding him he was *under condemnation*—and justly: "WE receive the due reward of our deeds: but this man hath done nothing amiss." See Romans 3:23.

2. A SINNER GETS A VISION OF CHRIST'S SAVING POWER. Luke 23:42—"LORD, remember me *when thou comest into thy kingdom.*" The cross was not to end in defeat for HIM.

He saw DIVINITY in that marred face, a *crown of crowns* in place of thorns, *a throne of majesty* instead of the accursed tree. He saw that Christ's crucifixion was not a FINALITY, but a STEP in the *redemption of the world:* John 3:16.

3. A SINNER SHOWS DEFINITE FAITH. Luke 23:42—"Remember ME." *Paradise with Christ* was assured him THAT VERY DAY: verse 43—"Jesus said unto him, Verily I say unto thee, TO DAY shalt thou be *with me in paradise.*"

Without church membership, baptism, money, good works—but on the basis of Ephesians 2:8-9—CALVARY PAYS. The cross is the plus sign of our minus lives.

29

Basic Requisites of Bible Study

ATTENTION-GETTER: YOU CAN'T MAKE ANY-
THING OUT OF THE BIBLE BY READING IT WITH
WOODEN SPECTACLES ON.

1. THERE MUST BE SPIRITUAL SIGHT.
*People may have very complete natural faculties of
mind,* but without inner illumination of the Holy Spirit,
they have *no capacity to understand spiritual truth.*

1 Corinthians 2:14—"The natural man receiveth not
the things of the Spirit of God: for they are *foolishness
unto him: neither can he know them,* because they are *spir-
itually discerned."*

There MUST be a SPIRITUAL BIRTH (John 3:5-7)
as the *first condition* of enjoyment in Bible study.

2. THERE MUST BE A DIVINE INSTRUCTOR. The
Bible is *never a dry Book to one who knows its AUTHOR*
(2 Timothy 3:16).

*The Author knows more about its meaning than any
man;* therefore, let us approach our study with the prayer
of Psalm 119:18.

No one can hope to understand everything all at once.
Leave the *difficulties* with Deuteronomy 29:29 until God
is pleased to give you better light. *Life's experiences* will
throw light on many *hard passages.* (See 1 John 2:27.)

3. THERE MUST BE A SURRENDERED STUDENT.

Bengal—"Apply thyself wholly to the scriptures—and—*apply the Scriptures* wholly to thyself." Psalm 119:33-34—"Teach me, O Lord, the way of thy statutes: . . . and *I shall keep thy law;* yea, *I shall observe it* with my *whole heart."*

God does not reveal His treasures to dishonest hearts. We get MORE light by *walking in the light we already have.*

Make every Bible FACT a FACTOR in your LIFE, and you will soon know the Bible is true. *Truth is lost, which ends merely in the knowing.*

REMEMBER: The degree of *spiritual discernment we have* will depend largely on *the habits of our souls*—the way we LIVE with reference to the *truth we already know* (1 Peter 1:22).

30

The Watered Garden of the Soul

ATTENTION-GETTER: GOD'S GREATEST BLESS-
INGS ARE FOR THOSE WHO ARE MORE CON-
CERNED ABOUT MAKING A LIFE THAN ABOUT
MAKING A LIVING.

Isaiah 58:10-11—"If thou *draw out thy soul to the hun-
gry,* and *satisfy the afflicted soul;* then shall thy *light rise*
in obscurity, and thy *darkness be as the noon day:* and the
LORD shall *guide thee* continually, and *satisfy thy soul* in
drought, and *make fat thy bones:* and thou shalt *be like a
watered garden,* and like a *spring of water,* whose waters
fail not."

NOTE TWOFOLD SECRET OF GUIDANCE: (a)
LOOKING to Him—Proverbs 3:6; (b) LIVING for
others—Scripture above.

*There is peril in being infatuated with truth and remain-
ing wholly inefficient.* Some talk of their enjoyment of
spiritual experiences but know nothing of the joy of SERV-
ICE in Christ's name.

When in doubt about your own way, begin to study how
you can *be a blessing to someone else.* Help the other person find his way. SEVEN things will result:

1. *Your own light will rise.* We can glorify God by

shining with the *feeble light we already have* (Matthew 5:16).

2. *Your darkness will give way to noonday.* Dispel your own by lightening the darkness of someone else.

3. *He will guide you continually.* The way to see farther ahead is to GO AHEAD as far as you can see your plain duty.

4. *Your own soul will be satisfied.* The thirst of your own heart is removed. See Psalm 63:1.

5. *Your bones will be made fat.* This means physical help. See Proverbs 11:25. *Forgetfulness of SELF* tends to all-around good health.

6. *Your life will be made like a watered garden.* Enlarge on this, comparing *flowers* and *fruits* to qualities of the *Spirit filled life.* See Psalms 1:2-3; 92:13-14.

7. *Your life watered by the Holy Spirit.* See Isaiah 12:3; John 7:37-39; 4:14.

31

Three Classes of Prayer Hindrances

ATTENTION-GETTER: PRAYER HAS TO COME
FROM THE ROOT OF THE HEART, NOT THE ROOF
OF THE MOUTH.

We are often beset by the question, WHY do I not seem
to have any power in prayer? There are THREE REALMS
in which we may look for CAUSES.

1. SINS of the FLESH. God said to some in Israel,
"When ye spread forth your hands, I will hide mine eyes
from you: yea, when ye make many prayers, I will not
hear (Isaiah 1:15).

WHY? *"Your hands are full of blood.* Wash you, *make
you clean;* put away the evil of your doings from before
mine eyes; cease to do evil" (vv. 15-16).

SOILED HANDS held up before God's face—this is
the BRAZENNESS of asking favors of Him when the
LIFE is full of wrongdoing. *"Sin is slapping God in the
face"*—A. J. Gordon.

If someone pulls down the telephone wire over which
you are speaking, you may keep talking but your message
will be *grounded.* Sin unconfessed *runs prayer into the
ground.* (See 1 John 1:9.)

2. SELF. James 4:3—"Ye ask, and receive not, because

ye ask amiss, that ye may consume it upon *your lusts {own desires}.*" SELF-CENTERED PRAYERS do not have the backing of the Holy Spirit.

Many who are well equipped to pray fail at this point: they do not *permit the Spirit* to frame their prayers (Romans 8:26). *Selfish prayers* are never effective. Prayer is as good as answered when it is clear to our hearts what GOD wants *us* to pray for.

3. SATAN. He is the great obstruction to prayer. *Read the experience of Daniel*—Daniel 10:1-14.

Paul shows us how *Satan concerns himself with the believer who seeks to rise into God's presence* (Ephesians 6:11-18). Often we have to battle with *unseen forces.* Only in the *energy of the Holy Spirit* can we do so—"IN THE SPIRIT" (v. 18). Satan cannot stand against *Spirit-taught* KNEE WORK in the *name of Jesus Christ.*

32

What Is Prayer?

ATTENTION-GETTER: PRAYER IS NOT JUST A DEVICE TO GET OUR WILLS DONE THROUGH HEAVEN.

> Prayer is the soul's sincere desire,
> Unuttered or expressed,
> The motion of a hidden fire,
> That trembles in the breast.
>
> JAMES MONTGOMERY

IN THE BIBLE SENSE, prayer is something *far more definite.* WISHES and ANXIETIES may *prepare* the heart for prayer, but they are *not effectual prayer* until they are ADDRESSED to God in the PRESCRIBED WAY.

John 14:13—the PROMISE does not apply to our *religious emotions,* but to OUR PETITIONS as God's CHILDREN, brought IN THE NAME of Jesus Christ our Saviour.

EVERY ONE OF THE ORIGINAL WORDS having to do with prayer has the *primary meaning* of TALKING to God: "Let your *requests be made known unto God"* (Philippians 4:6). *Express* the heart's desire.

PRAYER DEFINITIONS:

1. Beseeching *from* the Lord (Exodus 32:11).

68

2. Calling *upon* the Lord (Acts 7:59).
3. Crying *unto* the Lord (Exodus 22:23, 27).
4. Drawing *near* to the Lord (Psalm 73:28).
5. Seeking the *face* of the Lord (Psalm 27:8).
6. Lifting the heart *toward* the Lord (Lamentations 3:41).
7. Pouring out the soul *before* the Lord (Psalm 62:8).

NOTE ALWAYS the *element of approach* to and *address* to the PERSONAL heavenly Father—*not* just wishes, desires, or religious meditations.

James 5:16—"The effectual [lit., inwrought or energized] fervent prayer of a righteous man *availeth much.*" This is *praying in the energy of the Holy Spirit* (Ephesians 6:18).

Ephesians 2:18—"Through *him* [Christ] we . . . have access by one *Spirit* unto the *Father.*" (NOTE the *Trinity* of the Godhead involved in our prayers.)

PRAYER involves the USE OF WORDS. Hosea said, "Take with you WORDS, and turn to the LORD" (Hosea 14:2).

Do we allow the Holy Spirit to guide us in the WORDS we utter in prayer? See Romans 8:26.

33

"What Profit Shall We Have If We Pray?"

Job 21:15

ATTENTION-GETTER: ONE THING IS CERTAIN: GOD CANNOT DISAPPOINT DESIRES THAT ARE OF HIS OWN KINDLING.

John 14:14—"If ye shall ask, . . . I WILL DO." James 5:16—"The *effectual fervent* prayer of a righteous man *availeth* much."

What grounds of expectation do we have?

1. *Consider universal instinct.* "O thou that hearest prayer, unto thee shall all flesh come" (Psalm 65:2).

ALL MEN bow to *something* or *someone*. It is a demand of *human nature.* Scan the earth and see *people bowing to idols,* false gods, the unknown God, the God revealed in the Bible—in huts, under trees, in churches and cathedrals.

Unsaved people pray by INSTINCT (*atheists at sea,* people in *catastrophes*). WHEN SAVED, this becomes *intelligent principle* and the *prompting of the Holy Spirit.*

2. *Consider the nature of the personal God.* "If ye then, being evil, know how to give good gifts to your children, *how much more* shall your Father which is in heaven *give good things* to them that ask him?" (Matthew 7:11).

Has the Creator less interest in beings made in His image than *human parents* have in their offspring? Is the Creator *shut outside* as a mere spectator?

God has made millions of human beings *who are kind and considerate*. Is He Himself *without* these qualities? What about the *revelation of Himself in His Son, Jesus Christ?*

3. *Consider the revelation given in the Bible.* Quote several *prayer promises* (Matthew 6:6; Luke 11:9; John 14:13). "Call unto me, and *I will answer* thee, and show thee *great and mighty* things, *which thou knowest not*" (Jeremiah 33:3).

There is NO PSYCHOLOGY here—no "reflex action" from *concentrating the mind* on something *desired*. This is *divine intervention.*

If prayer IN JESUS' NAME *does not avail*, the promises are *mockery* and the injunctions to pray are *cruel deceit.*

PRAYER CHANGES THINGS. Cite definite answers.

34

Thanksgiving and Thanksliving

ATTENTION-GETTER: THERE ARE MANY WHO CRY "GOD BE MERCIFUL" BUT NEVER SAY "GOD BE PRAISED."

To be THANKFUL is to be MINDFUL of blessings received. There is MORE THANKS in the Bible than PRAYER.

THANKSGIVING should be the *accompaniment* of all prevailing prayer. Philippians 4:6—"Be careful [anxious] for nothing; but in *every thing* by prayer and supplication *with thanksgiving* let your requests be made known unto God."

RECKON UP the *temporal mercies* and *spiritual blessings* received. *How many times* have we returned thanks to God? Should we not be *as definite* in our THANKS as we are in our ASKING?

A man stranded on an island spent a whole day in *fasting* and *prayer* for deliverance. *None came.* The next day he decided to *spend in thanksgiving* on which he needed to catch up. A ship sighted him and picked him up.

WHEN PRAYING becomes up-hill work, *translate your blessings* into PRAISE for a while and *note the new power you* will have in PRAYER.

Thanksgiving in the Scriptures

It is GOOD: Psalm 92:1-2.

It is COMMANDED: Psalm 100:4; 1 Thessalonians 5:18.

It is MORE ACCEPTABLE than sacrifices: Psalm 29:30-31.

OUR LORD gave thanks: Matthew 11:25; John 11:41-42.

FAILURE to give thanks GRIEVES GOD: Luke 17:15-18.

Ingratitude BRINGS WRATH on men: Romans 1:18, 21.

FOR WHAT do we give thanks? Ephesians 5:20—"Giving thanks always for ALL things."

WHY should the Christian do this? Romans 8:28—He makes "ALL things" work together for good *to those who love Him.*

WHEN should we thank Him? 1 Thessalonians 2:13—We thank God "WITHOUT CEASING."

PRAYER may be offered for the last time—but PRAISE goes singing into HEAVEN. Read Revelation 5:13.

35

Christ's Testimony in Prayer

ATTENTION-GETTER: JESUS NEVER MADE A FALSE START ANY DAY OF HIS LIFE. HE BEGAN EVERY DAY BY LOOKING INTO HIS FATHER'S FACE.

1. *His earthly ministry began in prayer.* Luke 3:21— "Jesus . . . being baptized, AND PRAYING, the heaven was opened."

2. *It continued and ended in prayer.* Luke 23:34— "Father, forgive them; for they know not what they do."

3. *He was known for prayer from His youth.* John 11: 22—"I know, that even now, *whatsoever* thou wilt ask of God, God will give it thee."

4. *His heavenly ministry began in prayer.* John 14: 16—"I will pray the Father, and he shall give you another Comforter."

5. *He still continues as our intercessor.* Hebrews 7:25— "He ever liveth to make intercession for [us]."

LESSONS FROM HIS PRAYER LIFE

1. *He put it ahead of* PREACHING. Disciples asked Him how *to pray* (Luke 11:1) NOT how to PREACH. If we talk to God alone, we will have the right message.

Books and theology do not make preachers. PRAYER DOES.

2. *He put it ahead of* METHODS *in securing workers.* Matthew 9:38—"Pray ye therefore *the Lord* of the harvest, that HE will send forth labourers into his harvest." The Holy Spirit flows through MEN, not METHODS. *God-called men and women* is the need today.

3. *He put it ahead of rest.* Mark 1:35—"And in the morning, rising up *a great while before day,* he went out, and departed into a solitary place, *and there prayed."*

Great soul-winners are often *poor sleepers. Robert Mc-cheyne,* great Scottish soul-winner and preacher, *if he awoke in the night,* always got up to pray. *Samuel Rutherford met God at 3* A.M. *daily* to pray about his messages.

Luke 6:12—"It came to pass in those days, that he went out into a mountain to pray, and *continued all night* in prayer to God."

There will be little blessing on our work, unless we are first energized by prayer.

36

Abundant Life

ATTENTION-GETTER: GOD CALLS FOR THOSE
WHO HAVE NO MIGHT OR POWER BUT YEARN
TO BE FILLED WITH HIS POWER.

John 7:37-39—"In the last day, that *great* day of the
feast, Jesus stood and cried, saying, If any man *thirst*, let
him *come unto ME*, and *drink*. He that *believeth on me*,
as the scripture hath said, out of his *{innermost being}* shall
flow rivers of *living water*. (But this spake he of the Spirit,
which *they that believe on him* should receive: for the
Holy [Spirit] was not yet given; because that Jesus was not
yet glorified.)" (NOTE carefully WHO will receive the
Spirit.)

There are THREE great chapters in John on different
phases of the Holy Spirit's work:

Chapter 3—Spiritual life in its BEGINNING. *New
Birth* by the Spirit. INDWELLING. Review verses on
this.

Chapter 4—Spiritual life in its FULNESS. Review story
of the *woman at the well*. The INFILLING of the Spirit
for POWER.

Chapter 7—Spiritual life ABUNDANT for witnessing
and service. The OVERFLOWING life. Note CONDI-
TIONS of this life.

"Come unto ME" (John 7:37). This alone gives vital CONNECTION with the *Source* of the Stream. APPROACH to CHRIST—the *first essential.* (See 1 Corinthians 6:19-20.)

"Come . . . and DRINK." See closing book of the Bible (Revelation 22:17).

APPROPRIATION—Make the Holy Spirit active in your life by FULLY YIELDING to His control.

History clusters about the great water sources of earth. God's work centers about those who have the mighty refreshing of the Holy Spirit in their lives.

The RESULT is ABUNDANCE and OVERFLOW to bless others.

Remember: We are not RESERVOIRS of power—only AQUEDUCTS. *Dr. Archibald Brown,* when lauded for his great work, said, "Fifty-years ago, I was *joined onto the heavenly water main.* I've merely tried to *keep the tap open."*

37

To Me to Live Is Christ

Philippians 1:21

ATTENTION-GETTER: THE SECRET OF AN UN-SATISFIED LIFE IS A WILL NOT FULLY SURREN-DERED TO CHRIST.

In our Lord's intercessory prayer (John 17:23), He prayed that all His followers might be reproducers of His life from within—*"that the world may know* that thou hast sent me."

How can *the world* know what *Christ is like* except as *believers show* that He can make THEM like Himself?

1 John 2:6—"He that saith he abideth in him ought . . . to walk, even as HE walked." NOTE: None can follow such a PATTERN without a divine EMPOWERING (Philippians 4:13).

OUR RESPONSIBILITY is to respond to HIS ability (Galatians 2:20).

1. *Christ's Life Infused*

"I am the vine, *ye are the branches:* He that abideth in me, and I in him, the same *bringeth forth much fruit:* for [apart from] me ye can do nothing" (John 15:5).

Branches are the fruit-bearing part of the vine; but, only as the branch is able to receive the life-giving sap of the

78

vine, *can it produce.* There MUST BE this unhindered flow—through full yieldedness to Christ.

If we have given ourselves to HIM, we have no right to *deprive Him* of that which is *essentially His*—the means of *manifesting Himself* to others.

2. *Christ's Outshining*

"Now are ye light in the Lord: walk as children of light" (Ephesians 5:8). *We are diffusers of the light of Christ.* One who IS light is *penetrating the darkness* of this world, showing up SIN as a thing hateful to God and recommending the purity of Christ.

Philippians 2:15-16—"That ye may be blameless and harmless, the sons of God, without rebuke, in the midst of a crooked and perverse nation, among whom ye shine as [LUMINARIES] in the world; holding forth the word of life."

3. *Reflections of His Glory*

2 Thessalonians 1:12—"That the name of our Lord Jesus Christ may be glorified in you" (lit., "made all-glorious in you"). See Psalm 34:5: "They looked unto HIM and were RADIANT" (literal translation). Chinese converts named their missionary "Mr. GLORY-FACE."

38

Vital Salvation Truths

John 5:24

ATTENTION-GETTER: DO YOU KNOW THAT A PERSON MAY BE ALMOST SAVED, YET ENTIRELY LOST?

"Verily, verily, I say unto you, He that *heareth* my word, and *believeth* on him that sent me, *hath* everlasting life, and *shall not* come into condemnation [judgment]: but *is passed* from death *unto life*" (John 5:24).

When a verse begins with two verilys, watch for a *great packet of truth.* This passage is a DIAMOND of truth.

1. A New POSSESSION for the believer—*"everlasting life."* NOT just *eternal* EXISTENCE (ALL have that) but the LIFE OF GOD within eternal BLESSEDNESS (John 3:16).

"This is life eternal, that they might know thee, the only true God, and Jesus Christ, whom thou hast sent" (John 17:3). (Read also 1 John 5:11-18.)

2. A New PROVISION—"shall NOT come *into judgment"* (lit. meaning). *Judicially* our sins were *dealt with* by Jesus *on the cross* (1 Peter 2:24; Isaiah 53:6). When one believes, DESTINY is *settled,* because *Christ has taken* the believer's place. *A born-again* person CANNOT be called before the judgment bar *as to salvation.*

Believers WILL be judged concerning their WORKS, on which their REWARDS will be based (Romans 14: 10; 1 Corinthians 3:11-15).

3. A New POSITION—"passed from *death unto life.*" This means that the believer IS JUSTIFIED (Romans 5: 1). See Acts 13:39—"By HIM *all* that believe *are justified* [made as though they had never sinned] from *all things,* from which ye could not be justified by the law of Moses."

In the Person of our Substitute, the condemned sinner *died* for his sins *long ago;* and in THE RISEN CHRIST, he *came to life.* God sees him now in CHRIST in the heavenlies (Colossians 3:1-3).

How God deals with sin: Isaiah 38:17—cast *behind God's back;* Isaiah 44:22—"*blotted out,* as a thick cloud"; Psalm 103:12—"*far as the east is from the west";* Micah 7:19—"*Into the depths of the sea.*"

Have YOU claimed John 5:24 as YOUR OWN?

39

The Silence of Jesus

ATTENTION-GETTER: IF WE WOULD THINK TWICE BEFORE WE SPEAK, WE WOULD SPEAK TWICE BETTER FOR IT.

Spiritual strength consists of TWO things: (1) power of WILL and (2) power of SELF-RESTRAINT. Strong *feelings* and strong CONTROL over them.

COMPOSURE is often the result of the highest strength. *An important exhortation is "Rest* in the LORD, and *wait* patiently for *him"* (Psalm 37:7).

We lower ourselves and *grieve the Holy Spirit* by trying to *answer* bark with bark—*"blowing your top."*

THE STRENGTH OF JESUS

1. *Silent innocence.* Isaiah 53:7—"He was *oppressed,* and he was *afflicted,* yet he *opened not his mouth:* he is *brought as a lamb* to the slaughter, and *as a sheep* before her shearers is dumb, so *he openeth not his mouth."*

It would have been *irreparable loss to us* if he had *rebelled.* Oh, to know when it is GAIN to keep SILENT! There should be *silent acquiescence* to the will of God (Psalm 39:9).

2. *Silent under false accusation.* Matthew 27:12-14— "Then said Pilate unto him, Hearest thou not how many

things they witness against thee? And he *answered him to never a word."*

There was *no need to rehash* evidence that was FAKED. The very light on His face *showed Him incapable* of such things.

There is a time to maintain one's dignity (1 Peter 2: 19-20). To *answer back* would only *lower one.*

3. *Silent under rank injustice.* 1 Peter 2:23—"Who, when he was reviled, *reviled not again;* when he suffered, he *threatened not;* but committed himself to him that judgeth righteously."

True greatness is shown in ignoring undeserved abuse which ordinarily would set a man on fire.

> Silence my lips, Lord Jesus,
> Bid the tumult within be still,
> Quiet the raging billows,
> And my waiting soul infill.

AUTHOR UNKNOWN

40

The Citadel of the Christian

ATTENTION-GETTER: MAN'S GREATEST STRENGTH IS OFTEN SHOWN IN HIS ABILITY TO STAND AND TRUST.

"The *name of the* LORD is a *strong tower:* the righteous runneth into it, and is safe" (Proverbs 18:10).

We live in a world that is fatally ill. There is *"distress of nations,* with *perplexity"* (Luke 21:25). God's people will *feel the pressure* of the last days more and more.
BUT

His name is Wonderful (Isaiah 9:6); it is a *strong tower* to His people. "LORD" of the Old Testament is the "CHRIST" of the New Testament. HIS is the *"name* which is *above every name"* (Philippians 2:9), by which we can approach Almighty God at any moment.

Here is our TOWER that cannot be destroyed by any human artillery or device of atheists—or combined powers of darkness.

It is for THE RIGHTEOUS. (See 2 Corinthians 5:21; Romans 3:21-22.)

1. TOWER OF SAFETY from the merited *penalty of sin.* "Tower of SALVATION"—2 Samuel 22:51. Years ago *a carpenter, Edward Mote* recently saved, *walked a*

London street, thinking of the *power Christ* had manifested *in his life* in so short a time. Some *words came to him.* He stopped and *jotted them down:* "My hope is built on nothing less, than Jesus' blood and righteousness. I dare not trust the sweetest frame, but *wholly lean on Jesus' name."* WHAT A TOWER OF SAFETY!

2. TOWER OF REFUGE from besetting FEARS. 2 Samuel 22:3—"He is ... my *high tower* and my *refuge, my Saviour;* thou savest me *from violence."*

In India burdens are carried on heads. Resting stones are placed along the road, upon which one may deposit his load while resting. A *native convert said,* "Christ is now *my rest-Stone."*

3. TOWER SET ALOFT—*to give us a vantage point.* Psalm 18:2—"The LORD is ... my HIGH tower." He lifts us up beyond the reach of arrows. Let Him lift you into *"the heavenlies"* (Ephesians 1:3).

41

Heaven in the Home

ATTENTION-GETTER: EDGAR GUEST SAID, "IT TAKES A HEAP OF LIVING IN A HOUSE TO MAKE IT A HOME."

One of the most suggestive types of HEAVEN is a Christian home on earth. The home of which *Christ is the Head* should be *next to heaven* in our thoughts.

The Christian's earthly home should be the very VESTIBULE of heaven. It *should* be but *a step from the one home to the other.* "Surely goodness and mercy shall follow me all the days of my life: and I will dwell in the *house of the* LORD *for ever*" (Psalm 23:6).

HOW CAN WE HAVE SUCH HOMES?

1. Read Joshua 24:14-15. The BEGINNING is in a *solemn covenant* between husband and wife to make CHRIST the *Head* of the home.

NOTE: Children will have a *slim chance of spiritual progress* when father or mother are *not* consistently *leading the way* in this resolution.

The first responsibility of man and wife to SOCIETY is to establish *a Christian home*—with thanks at meals, daily *devotions*, Christian *habits*.

86

One may have a modest home; but if Christ is the HEAD, *more happiness can be generated* in it than in the *finest mansion* in which there is *no place for Him.*

2. Psalm 101:2—"I will walk *within my house* with a *perfect heart."* Let husband and wife *sincerely determine* that they will be *living exemplifications* of Christian teaching.

A Chinese Christian boy said, "I am reading my Bible and BEHAVING it." If we are OBEYING it, we will *start each day with the prayer* that Christ will regulate all our habits and pursuits and be the solution of every problem that arises.

A little boy asked his father what kind of a man a Christian is. He tried to explain, but what a stab in the heart he felt when the lad suddenly asked, "Have I ever SEEN one?"

Keep HOME near HEAVEN so all will know that there is heaven in your home.

42

Let the Redeemed of the Lord Say So

Psalm 107:2

ATTENTION-GETTER: LITTLE SENTENCES SPO-
KEN EARNESTLY FOR JESUS SAVE SOULS.

"I am *not ashamed* of the gospel of Christ: for it is the
power [DYNAMITE] of God unto salvation to every one
that believeth" (Romans 1:16).

Satan is supersensitive about one thing—saved people
beginning to witness to others about Christ's saving power.

The Bible presents the power of WITNESS as most pro-
found and puts upon every Christian *the responsibility* of
speaking out for Christ. Let's see what it says:

1. *Testifying is the first evidence of a saving experience.*
Romans 10:9-10—ESSENTIAL ACCOMPANIMENT of
salvation.

Christ has NO SILENT PARTNERS. While salvation
belongs first in the heartbeats of one's *affections,* the heart
that *has taken* Jesus will not *lock the door* and try to *keep
Him there* without sharing Him.

"Out of the abundance of the *heart,* the *mouth* speaketh"
(Luke 6:45). It is the NORMAL answer of a new-born
soul. *What closes one's mouth?* Read Proverbs 29:25;
John 12:42-43.

2. *Testifying is vital to one's own spiritual development.*
Revelation 12:11—"They overcame him [Satan] by the
blood of the Lamb, *and* by the *word of their testimony."*
Proverbs 3:6—"In all thy ways *acknowledge him,* and he
shall direct thy paths."

The leanest souls among Christians are those who try
to keep a MONOPOLY on their blessings. Every time we
speak out for Christ, we *make it harder for temptation* to
get us. Telling others what God has done *increases* and
establishes convictions, develops faith. (Compare *Peter*—
Matthew 26:69-75 and Acts 2:22-36.)

3. *Loyalty to Christ DEMANDS testimony.* Matthew
10:32-33. *We can't be silent* about Him in a world that
is *against Him a*nd count ourselves *true to Him.* Read
Psalm 119: 46 as a RESOLUTION.

43

Have You Lost the Lord?

ATTENTION-GETTER: IF YOU HAD LOST THE
LORD, WHERE WOULD YOU LOOK FOR HIM?

John 20:13—"They have *taken away my Lord,* and I
know not where they have laid him."

Many, like Mary, under the pressure of trial and sorrow,
become bewildered and benumbed, and cannot seem to lo-
cate their Lord. Have YOU been *losing the sense of His
presence?*

Where do you think you broke company with Him?
There are usually TWO places where we *could have parted*
with Him. *Go back to those places* and INVESTIGATE.

1. The place of NEGLECTED PRAYER. Luke 18:1—
"Men ought ALWAYS to pray, and *not to faint."*

Prayer is the strategic point Satan always watches. If he
can get us to become *perfunctory in our prayer,* we will
soon *neglect prayer altogether.*

Cold-hearted, formal, feeble prayers will not suffice when
swirling currents of trial and temptation come our way.
If we do not pray when the sun shines, we will find ourselves *unable* to find Him *in the darkness.*

Come back to Philippians 4:6-7 and recover "the peace
of God, which passeth all understanding.

2. The place of FORGOTTEN PROMISES. Psalm 27:

13—"I had fainted, unless *I had believed to see* the goodness of the LORD in the land of the living." He always keeps His promises.

Samuel Rutherford: "Whenever I find myself in the *cellars of affliction,* I look around for the *King's wine bottles* [promises] and drink rich draughts of vitalizing grace."

Our PRAYERS have to have SUPPORT. *Meditation* on His PROMISES brings the sense of His PRESENCE.

David in Psalm 61:2—"Lead me to the rock that is higher than I." The PROMISES ever stand above the tide. Make it to some solid promises and hang on. You will find the sense of the Lord's nearness to you.

44

Wit's End Corner

Psalm 107:27

ATTENTION-GETTER: DO YOU BELIEVE IN
THE SUN WHEN IT IS PITCH DARK?

We are always getting ourselves into TIGHT COR-
NERS (coming to our *"wit's end"*). The Bible has just
such an *expression* and shows us how *God makes full provision* for His children who need more than human wisdom.

The apostle Paul FIVE times uses *a Greek word* which
means "in a *tight corner,*" or, as we would say, "at our *wit's
end.*" Note these passages and see how God always opened
the *way of escape.*

1. 2 Corinthians 6:3-7. In the midst of a long list of
hectic circumstances faced by Paul, he says (v. 4) "In all
things approving ourselves [or, demonstrating our confi-
dence] . . . in DISTRESSES" (lit., when in TIGHT COR-
NERS).

We do not need to be panicky: His grace will enable us
to *commend ourselves* and to have a *victorious testimony,*
even when it appears, humanly speaking, that there is NO
WAY OUT.

2. 2 Corinthians 4:8-11. "We are troubled on every side, yet not DISTRESSED" (v. 8) Lit., "not *completely cornered.*" Rotherham trans., *"not hemmed in."*

No tight corner can hold us if CHRIST is with us in it. Wit's end corner is a *blessing in disguise,* if it *presses us nearer* to Him.

3. 2 Corinthians 12:9-10. "I take pleasure in . . . DISTRESSES [lit., tight corners] *for Christ's sake:* for when I am weak, then am I strong" (v. 10).

God plans nothing less than our completeness and holiness. He *knows what process to use.* We need never be morbid.

4. Romans 8:35-37. "Who shall separate us from the love of Christ? shall . . . DISTRESS [lit., *being in tight corners}? . . .* Nay, in all these things we are *more than conquerors* through him that loved us."

One who is sheltered under His love finds *God's worst* better than the devil's best. DISAPPOINTMENT is His APPOINTMENT. Glorious victory is assured those who love Him—*in His good time.*

45

Notable Three: Sixteens

ATTENTION-GETTERS: DID YOU EVER GO ON
A 3:16 HUNT IN YOUR NEW TESTAMENT?

We are accustomed to John 3:16 as the *Golden Text*
of the New Testament, but there are *other* 3:16s that are
spiritual treasures.

1. 2 Timothy 3:16—"All scripture is given by inspiration of God, and is profitable for doctrine, for reproof, for
correction, for instruction in righteousness."

The word for "inspiration" means *"God-breathed."* The
writers of Scripture were persons *qualified by the Holy
Spirit* to receive and communicate *divine truth,* as they
wrote *in the original* Hebrew or Greek.

2. John 3:16—"For God so loved the world, that he
gave his only begotten Son, that whosoever believeth in
him should not perish, but have everlasting life."

Twenty-five words in English! Who put such *undying
words* together? *Millions* have had their lives *transformed*
by receiving *these golden words* in childlike faith, in all
parts of the earth.

3. 1 John 3:16—"Hereby perceive we the *love of God,
because he laid down his life* for us."

This involves the fact that "the Word was *made flesh,*
and dwelt among us (John 1:14). HE, *God's Son,* went to

94

the *depths of Calvary* (Philippians 2:6-9). We *know nothing* of the love of God *until* we see it through the *window of the cross.*

4. Colossians 3:16—"Let the word of Christ dwell in you richly in all wisdom."

Does the world know *anything more wonderful* than His words (John 6:63)? *What a spiritual force* they have been in the world for two thousand years!

Spurgeon reckoned it the *greatest compliment* of his life when *a scoffer* said, "Here he is, after nineteen centuries, still teaching *the musty doctrine* of a Nazarene carpenter." There is *nothing more enriching* in life today than the words of Jesus Christ.

Close with Paul's wonderful PRAYER for us all in Ephesians 3:16. Have YOU tapped these mighty resources in the risen Christ?

Subjects

(By theme numbers)